Discovering Mexican Cooking

Good health and good eating!

Alice Erie Young

Patricia Peters Stephenson

Discovering Mexican Cooking

by
ALICE ERIE YOUNG
PATRICIA PETERS STEPHENSON

Illustrations by
PATRICIA PETERS STEPHENSON

Advisor on Mexican Foods and Customs
THEODOSIA MORENO SAMANO

The Naylor Company
Publishers of the Southwest
San Antonio, Texas

DEDICATED
to our families
and our friends

Contents

*Quick tips to those of you who don't have time really to discover Mexican cooking!

Foreword

We Live in the Southwest!

And we like Mexican food! It is fun to eat it in a Mexican restaurant; it is also fun to serve at home. Mexican food is inexpensive, and so adaptable to informal entertaining.

We feel that between us we represent YOU, our readers, for

AL, THE AUTHOR, has never been farther into Mexico than the border towns, so she is truly "discovering".

PAT, THE ILLUSTRATOR, traveled in Mexico and is a teacher of Home Economics as well!

THEO, THE ADVISOR, lived in Mexico for thirty years and for five years owned and operated a restaurant in Jacala, Hidalgo.

Mexico

Land of Ancient Civilizations, Folk Arts, Fiestas, and FOOD! There must be a background to it all, SO WE HAD . . .

— (Peter Balestrero, Western Ways)

Al   Theo   Pat

*C*onversations

Our first conversations seemed more like conferences. Laden with maps and notebooks, we would gather in the living room of Mrs. Sámano's home.

AL: Which foods are *really* Mexican?

THEO: Corn . . . chile . . . chocolate . . . tomatoes . . . beans. Even in pre-conquest times, these were the native foods. Corn was so filling and satisfying . . . and kept indefinitely, too. When wandering tribes began to settle down in order to raise it, civilization began.

PAT: In 1517, when Cortés and his Spanish adventurers invaded Mexico in search of gold and silver, the Aztec leader, Montezuma, used these foods as gifts

10

to them. Cortés was so impressed he sent the foods back to Spain.

AL: What did the Spaniards bring?

THEO: They brought livestock, such as goats, cattle, sheep, pigs . . . also, wheat, rice, almonds, olives, eggs, chickens. From these the Mexicans made bread, soups, stews, cheese, omelets, and custards.

AL: Do the Mexicans use any spice but chile?

THEO: Yes, they use many herbs and spices, such as OREGANO, CUMIN, BAYLEAF; and in desserts and beverages, CINNAMON, NUTMEG, CLOVE, and MINT. And, of course, CLOVE of GARLIC!

PAT: Do you ever substitute GARLIC POWDER or GARLIC SALT for garlic?

THEO: Yes, GARLIC POWDER is finely ground dehydrated garlic. I allow ⅛ teaspoon for each clove of garlic; or if I use GARLIC SALT, I reduce the amount of regular salt by one-half. And today garlic oil and garlic puree can also be bought.

PAT: The Mexicans use lard for frying. Do you ever use vegetable oils?

THEO: Yes, and bacon drippings, too. Or olive oil.

PAT: I've noticed when we order a Mexican plate in this country, or when we serve it in our homes, we put all the food on one plate. Why don't the Mexicans do this?

THEO: It may be our streamlined way of doing things. However, the Mexicans prefer to eat each food separately.

AL: How often do they eat?

THEO: First thing in the morning they have a pre-breakfast called DESAYUNO of hot spiced chocolate and *pan dulce,* a sugared bun; in the middle of the morning, breakfast or ALMUERZO includes eggs, sausage or *chorizo,* tortillas, refried beans, and coffee. In the middle of the day they have a lunch or COMIDA CORRIDA . . . two soups, vegetables, refried beans, tortillas, and perhaps a custard dessert. After a siesta, tea or MERIENDA. Late in the evening, dinner or CENA is served with meats, fish, tortillas or bread,

11

coffee, and dessert of pastries. The Mexicans really love to eat!

AL: If tortillas are so popular, don't they know about wheat bread?

THEO: Yes, for they always eat *pan dulce,* a sugared bun, with their coffee or chocolate.

PAT: What short cuts can we take and still serve a nice Mexican dinner?

THEO: We can take advantage of our labor-saving devices like blenders, mixers, deep-fat fryers. We can prepare the meal ahead of time and freeze it. We can also get part of our ingredients out of cans.

AL: Well . . . where shall we start the cookbook?

THEO: I think you should start with . . .

Corn

Tortillas

Quesadillas

Tostadas

Tacos

Enchiladas

Tamales

Corn

Corn is the basis of the most popular Mexican recipes. According to Toltec legend, Quetzalcoatl, their most important god, helped them discover corn, and establish a prosperous civilization, but because of

13

jealousy, Quetzalcoatl was forced to leave. However, he promised to return.

Later, the Aztecs, who replaced the Toltecs in the Valley of Mexico, thought Cortés to be the returning Quetzalcoatl. Cortés arrived in 1517, destroyed and enslaved the Aztec Empire, and Spanish colonization began. This resulted in the blending of the cultures that are now Mexican.

Masa

MASA is corn dough. It spoils easily, so must be ground fresh and used within a few days. In the picture below, dried corn is being prepared in the traditional way. Put 5 to 7 lbs. corn and 1 cup lime in large jar or OLLA . . . cover with cold water and place over low fire. When it starts to boil, take off the fire and cover to cool. Rinse thoroughly, rub between hands so all the lime and the little yellow skins are washed off. Now it is NIXTAMAL.

On the right, NIXTAMAL is mixed with water

from the pitcher or JARRO, ground by hand to a smooth paste on a stone METATE with a MANO. Now it is MASA.

Roll the MASA into a ball, pat it round and thin, cook on a COMAL (the straw fan or AVENTADOR is used to fan the flame, if necessary). Cook it lightly on one side (less than a minute), flip to other side and when done, flip it back and finish the first side. Now it is a TORTILLA.

Sounds simple? Remember the secret ingredient is called SKILL! However . . .

Tortillas

Tortillas may be bought MACHINE made . . . are inexpensive and satisfactory to use because of uniform size. You can buy them in a Mexican store, or in packages or cans in a supermarket.

There are two kinds:

1. Tortillas de Maíz, corn, page 16.

2. Tortillas de Harina, wheat flour, page 19.

TO FRESHEN . . . steam tortillas (without getting them soggy) by dampening, if necessary, and heating on ungreased griddle or in bun warmer, or place in oven in aluminum foil.

TO STORE in refrigerator or freezer . . . wrap securely, as they dry out easily.

TO SERVE at the table . . . keep hot in napkin like hot biscuits. Each person should butter and roll his own . . . and let the butter drip!

Gordita

Gordita, "little fat one," a thicker tortilla.

Raspada

Raspada, the face or front side of a tortilla. It peels off easily.

Tostada

Tostada, toasted (fried) corn tortilla, page 18.

Tortillas de Maíz

There is a good masa flour on the market . . . handy because it is dehydrated . . . *proportions for masa on package*: 2 cups MASA HARINA, 1⅓ cups warm water.

To Make Corn Tortillas: (Approximately 12)

We like this recipe because the salt and shortening make the tortillas more tasty.

2 cups Masa Harina	2½ cups boiling
1½ t. salt	water
1 T. shortening	

Mix dry ingredients in bowl. Melt shortening in the boiling water and add to ingredients. Stir to make a stiff dough, using a spoon or mixer (2 minutes at medium speed).

Four Methods of Shaping Tortillas

1. Traditional method, page 14.

2. Put ball of dough, about 1 inch in size, between damp muslin. Press with flat surface as a plate . . . don't add flour. The tricky part is to get it off the muslin. SO, peel back the top muslin from the tortilla, and get it in your hand.

3. Use rolling pin and muslin.

4. Use TORTILLA PRESS, two boards hinged together, faced with galvanized iron, with press-down lever. Place ball of dough between damp muslin before putting in the press.

To Cook Tortillas:

Have slightly greased griddle very hot. Half-cook one side of tortilla (less than a minute), turn it over and cook for about a minute until it gets nicely brown in several spots, then turn again. When it puffs up, press down with pancake turner!

Quesadillas

For individual serving:

1 uncooked corn   1 slice cheese
  tortilla

Place cheese on tortilla, fold over, and press edge. It looks like a turnover. Cook lightly on hot ungreased griddle, or broil, or deep fry (375°) until golden brown, and cheese is melted.

Variation:

On uncooked corn tortilla, put a tablespoon of filling such as refried beans, chile con carne (chile sauce with meat), or  chicken. Add cheese, fold over, and press edge. Deep fry (375°) until brown and crisp (about 4 minutes). If desired, serve with Red Chile Sauce, page 25, or canned Enchilada Sauce.

For Colorful Quesadillas:

When making corn tortillas (page 16), use 2 cups boiling Red Chile Sauce (canned Enchilada Sauce) instead of the boiling water. These will be delicately flavored and have a red-orange color!

17

Tostadas de Maíz

Deep fry corn tortillas until crisp. These can be frozen. Reheat in oven as needed.

Cut tortilla into 4 pieces, deep fry. Use in place of crackers with soup, beans, or salad. For a special treat, spread with *guacamole,* page 37.

Crushed

Crush crisp fried tortillas, and use instead of cracker crumbs in casseroles.

Rolled

Fry tortilla lightly so it stays soft (see TO COOK TORTILLAS, page 17).
Fill, and roll for rolled enchiladas, page 27.

Folded

For Taco Shells

Fry tortilla crisp in deep fat (can be done in as little as 1/2″ fat, but turn the taco from side to side as you crisp it), keeping it curved or U-shaped, rather than sharp or V-shaped. Use kitchen tongs to hold one side while frying, so it won't close.

A Taco Maker

Some people like to use a TACO MAKER, a mold to hold the tortilla properly as it is frying . . . two bent pieces of metal, tortilla-sized, one fitting inside the other. Place tortilla between the metal. You could make your own from a large tin can . . . cut two circles, perforate, and bend.

Tortillas de Harina   (1 dozen)

These are made with white (*wheat*) flour.

2 cups white flour	1 T. shortening
½ t. salt	¼ cup hot water

Sift flour and salt. Add shortening and mix well before adding water. Knead until springy and elastic.

To shape tortillas, see FOUR METHODS, page 16. If made by experts, a tortilla may be three feet across, and will look like thin wet silk as it is gracefully tossed, stretched, and pulled into shape. If baking powder is added (1 teaspoon for above recipe), the tortilla won't stretch . . . so will be smaller-sized.

Tostadas de Harina

Crisp flour tortillas in buttered skillet until speckled. Spread with butter, and put in oven to melt butter. OR, spread with butter and grated cheese, and put in oven to melt the cheese.

Tacos

Tacos are fried, filled corn tortillas. They are the most widely used Mexican food in the United States.

Crisp and Folded Tacos

Delightful to serve for a crowd because easy for the hostess. The tortillas can be fried early and set into

a large pan. For folding tortillas, see page 18. The ingredients can be lined up ready to be placed in the taco shells at the last minute.

The Taco Line-Up of Fillings

The meat* in tacos is often beef. Ground beef can be fried or broiled, and Red Chile Sauce (Enchilada Sauce) added. For variety, try pieces of cooked beef, or chicken, or ham. An all vegetable filling such as cooked peas, carrots, etc., is delicious, too.

*Meat   Toss as for salad: Grated cheese   (Enchilada Sauce) Red Chile Sauce

shredded lettuce   sliced radishes
chopped onion   pinch of oregano
sliced ripe or green olives

Soft and Rolled Tacos

For this taco, use corn tortillas, fresh or steamed (page 16). They must be pliable so they will not crack when rolled. Sometimes we omit frying the tortilla lightly, and just fill and roll it.

Fry lightly   Fill   Roll

Variation:

Instead of cheese and lettuce *topping,* use mashed avocado (*guacamole,* page 37), OR sour cream (*jocoque*) . . .

Crisp and Flat Tacos

Fry corn tortilla crisp and flat. Serve whole, spread thinly with refried beans (page 33) and any other taco filling you desire (page 20). Top with shredded lettuce.

Crisp and Rolled Tacos

Spread corn tortilla with meat filling, roll. Fry until crisp. Drain on absorbent paper. To serve, garnish with salad mixture and cheese.

La Tostada Grande

A nibbling good centerpiece served on a large tin cake stand in Mexican restaurants!

This is a tostada made of the large tortilla described on page 19. You can serve it at home — IF you have a griddle three feet wide!

Chile

The Mexicans grind their chiles on volcanic stone in a bowl or *molcajete* or on a flat *metate*.

Ground

We can buy ground chile in bulk or in small packages in a Mexican store or in a supermarket. Like all ground spices, it loses its flavor quickly.

Powder

Chile Powder is a well-known condiment blend of chiles, cumin seed, marjoram, bay leaves, cloves, garlic.

Paste

Buy it already prepared! *To make it . . .* open dry chile peppers, remove seeds and membranes, steam to soften, scrape pulp from skins. OR add a little liquid to pure ground chile.

Liquid

RED CHILE SAUCE (or Enchilada Sauce), canned, is the best to use. It may have a little olive oil, vinegar, garlic, spices in it.

CHILE SAUCE with TOMATO, canned or bottled, much milder because the tomato, is like catsup.

HOT SAUCE in bottle . . . made of small, red, hot peppers, as Tabasco, so is very hot.

23

Chile Peppers

All the many varieties of chile peppers (and common bell peppers, pimento, paprika, cayenne) are of the same species, *Capsicum frutescens.*

The best known of the red chiles are Chile *ancho,* a dark red . . . Chile *pasilla,* long, very dark . . .Chile *mulato,* smaller, rounder.

Chile peppers give colorful, flavorful, distinctive piquancy to Mexican cooking. Chiles vary in size from 1/4" to 6". The seeds and membrane holding them are the hottest part of the pepper. Also, the smaller the hotter . . . so watch out for Chiles *Tepines,* size of a pea, or Chiles *Jalapeños,* an inch long.

A typical part of Mexican homes is the decorative strings or *ristras* of long red chiles hanging on the adobe walls. Actually this may be the Mexican's supply of chile for the year. Chiles may be picked green, or if allowed to ripen will turn red or yellow, depending on the kind.

NOTE: On some labels you will find chile spelled with an "i" . . . *chili.*

Chile Verde (green)

EASIEST . . . to buy canned!

A 4-oz. *can* of PEELED GREEN CHILE PEPPERS contains about 5 of the 6" chile peppers, flattened and folded . . . so don't let the small size of the can fool you! Before using, *rinse* the chiles and *remove seeds and membranes.* Use in Green Chile *Relish (Salsa de Chile Verde),* page 25, *Chiles Rellenos,* page 26, and *Sopa de Chile Verde,* page 35.

FRESH GREEN CHILES to be properly prepared are blistered and peeled . . . a job for an expert.

Chile Sauces

The most common kinds of chile peppers used in making fresh chile sauces are Chile *ancho*, Chile *pasilla*, or Chile *mulato*. OR maybe you have a chile pepper plant in your home and don't realize its possibilities! To make tomato sauce, get one chile from your plant, mash it with a little garlic, onion, and tomato. Delicious! And the more peppers you pick, the more you'll grow!

Red Chile Sauce (makes 2 cups)

(For canned Red Chile Sauce, see page 23)

½ T. fat
1 T. flour
2 T. chile powder or
  1 cup chile paste
1 cup canned tomatoes, strained
1 t. vinegar

2 cups, or 1 can beef
  or chicken broth
1 small onion,
  chopped
1 clove of garlic,
  mashed
salt and pepper to taste

Brown fat and flour in saucepan. Add chile powder or chile paste, strained tomatoes, vinegar, broth, and stir until a smooth gravy mixture. Add onion and garlic. Season well. Simmer for about 3 minutes.

Green Chile Relish (Salsa de Chile Verde)

You can buy it!

3 green chile peppers
  (canned, see page 24)
3 peeled tomatoes or
  1½ cups tomatoes,
  strained (If you
  like milder relish,
  add more tomato)

2 small green onions
1 t. vinegar
1 clove of garlic,
  minced, if desired
salt to taste

Continued

Chop chile peppers, tomatoes, and onions. Add rest of ingredients and mix thoroughly.

Mole Sauce

Mole Sauce is served over meat or fowl, especially turkey. To make Mole, add these ingredients to Red Chile Sauce, page 25.

Grind and stir until well blended:

⅓ cup almonds	⅓ stick cinnamon
1 T. peanuts or peanut butter	2 slices toast
	3 corn tostadas
2 t. caraway seed	1 oz. bitter chocolate
½ t. cloves	1 medium onion

Add . . .

½ cup strained tomatoes	1 clove of garlic, mashed

Simmer for 30 minutes until it is a thick sauce.

Chiles Rellenos (Stuffed Chiles)   6 servings

The omelets may be prepared early, then heated in oven before serving.

Chiles:

1 4 oz. can peeled green chiles (see page 24)	6 1 inch cubes cheese

Place cube of cheese in center of each chile.

Batter:

3 egg whites	3 T. flour
3 egg yolks	

26

Beat egg whites to soft peaks. Beat egg yolks, and combine with flour and fold into egg whites.

Omelets:

In greased griddle, make six ovals of batter, place a stuffed chile on each oval, and cover with more batter. Brown on both sides. Cover each omelet with heated SAUCE and Serve.

Sauce:

2 medium onions, chopped	1 8 oz. can tomato sauce
2 cloves of garlic, minced	$\frac{1}{2}$ cup water
2 T. flour	$\frac{1}{4}$ t. oregano
	$\frac{1}{2}$ t. salt

Brown onions, garlic, and flour in hot fat. Add tomato sauce, water, oregano, salt. Simmer about 15 minutes.

Enchiladas

Enchiladas are corn tortillas covered with Red Chile Sauce (Enchilada Sauce).

Rolled (6 servings)

12 corn tortillas
1 can Red Chile Sauce (Enchilada Sauce)
12 $\frac{1}{2}$" cubes cheese or 1 cup cooked meat

chopped onion to garnish
grated cheese to garnish

Continued

Fry corn tortillas lightly so they stay soft. Dip quickly into hot Red Chile Sauce. (If tortilla breaks when you dip it, spread the sauce on with a spoon.) Fill with cheese or a spoonful of cooked meat, and roll. Place rolled enchiladas close together in baking dish. Pour some Red Chile Sauce over each roll and top with chopped onion and grated cheese. Place in hot oven to melt cheese.

Stacked (3 layers to a stack)

Fry corn tortillas crisp and flat. Dip each tortilla into hot Red Chile Sauce (Enchilada Sauce). Place one or more of the following fillings between each layer:

refried beans, page 33
cooked meat
grated cheese
chopped onion
shredded lettuce

And these, also, if you like:

sliced radishes
sliced tomatoes

sliced ripe or green olives

Tamales

Tamales are masa dough spread on corn husks topped with a spoonful of filling, then rolled and steamed. They are reserved for really festive occasions. It takes time to make them BUT it is really worth the effort. Maybe you don't like tamales, and perhaps the reason is that you have never tasted a GOOD one! We think this is a GOOD RECIPE for tamales.

Your shopping list:
This recipe makes about 36 tamales, depending on the size of the corn husks. We suggest you make a quan-

tity of tamales and freeze some of them by wrapping individually in foil. To serve: place in foil in oven until heated through.

CORN HUSKS — buy ½ lb. clean, large, golden corn husks at a Mexican store. You *could* cut the husks from mature corn, and dry until golden (these will not be as large or as satisfactory). Do not use parchment.

MEAT — 5 lbs. Beef (chuck or flank), or pork, or chicken, or a combination of beef and pork. Plan to have 1 quart of meat after cooking.

RED CHILE SAUCE (Enchilada Sauce) — 2 (10 oz.) cans. Buy extra if you like to serve sauce at the table.

GROUND CHILE — 1 package. You will use about ⅓ cup. This will be added to the Red Chile Sauce. Seasoning in tamales must be hotter because some flavor is lost when steamed next to the *masa* dough.

OLIVES — green, pitted, 1 jar or can.

MASA — 4 lbs. (8 cups) of fresh *masa* at a Mexican store. If you use MASA HARINA (page 16) buy 1 package. You will need 6 cups. Do not substitute corn meal or hominy for *masa*, as it is not the same.

GREEN CORN TAMALES listed in "season only" on menus, are made of fresh, *fully ripe* (late summer) white corn. The kernels must be cut off and taken to a mill to be ground into a paste. *To make green corn tamales*: on green corn husks, first spread the paste, then top with strips of green chile and some cheese. The husks are then folded and steamed.

The Steamer

Prepare your Steamer — If you don't have a steamer, use a large kettle, or a pressure cooker (15 lbs., 25 minutes). The procedure is the same. Turn another pan upside-down in it to keep water line from touching the tamales. Cover with small pieces of corn husk. Remember when you are filling the steamer or kettle with tamales, keep them from tipping by putting a jar or can in the center.

Tamale Method:

Meat — Cook in small amount of water until very tender. Add salt to taste.

Corn husks — Rinse and soak in hot water until pliable. Drain thoroughly. Save small pieces for lining the steamer.

Prepare Masa Dough, using Masa

4 lbs. (8 cups) Masa	3 T. plus 1 t. baking powder
4 cups broth or water	
1 lb. lard	3 t. salt

using dry Masa Harina (page 16)

6 cups dry Masa Harina	1 lb. lard
6 cups warm broth or water	3 T. plus 1 t. baking powder
	3 t. salt

Combine *masa* with broth, mixing with hands into soft dough. Add more liquid, if necessary.

Add salt and baking powder to lard. Mix thoroughly (easy in an electric mixer). Add *masa* dough. Beat until VERY fluffy and easy to spread. You are trying to get air into the dough. You can't beat it too much. *Water test* — drop a bit of dough in water, if it floats it is done.

Mix 2 10 oz. cans Red Chile Sauce, and 1/3 cup ground chile with the meat, simmer 5 minutes. You may want to add a little more ground chile (mix with a little water) to be sure the chile flavor is much stronger than you usually expect it to be. Some of the strength is lost when steamed next to the masa dough.

Open small jar or can of olives. Prepare steamer, see page 29.

Tamale Assembly Line

husks

masa dough

meat & chile

olives

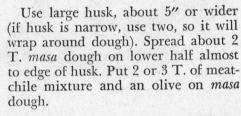

Use large husk, about 5″ or wider (if husk is narrow, use two, so it will wrap around dough). Spread about 2 T. *masa* dough on lower half almost to edge of husk. Put 2 or 3 T. of meat-chile mixture and an olive on *masa* dough.

Fold one side over, then fold the second side over a little past the middle. It will hold together because of the *masa* dough.

Fold end up. Place folded end down in steamer. Be careful it doesn't tip.

Put husks on top of filled steamer. Cover, and s t e a m about 45 minutes, or until *masa* dough peels away from corn husk. Don't let the steamer boil dry. If pressure c o o k e r is used, 15 lbs. for 25 minutes.

SERVE tamales peeled, or in husks at the table. Serve some extra sauce, too.

BUENOS TAMALES!

$\mathcal{B}$eans (Frijoles)

Beans rank with corn as the staple food of Mexico
. . . are rich in many nutrients including iron and
vitamin B. The Mexicans never add chile to beans . . .
that is a variation popular in the U. S. The type of bean
grown in Mexico varies in color and size because of
the regional conditions. In this country, we use a
mottled bean called pinto . . . reminding one of a
pinto horse. When the beans are cooked, these spots
disappear.

To Cook Frijoles (12 servings)

1 lb. pinto beans   1 T. fat, or small
2 qts. water   piece of salt pork
1 T. salt

Wash beans and soak overnight in water. Simmer in covered pan for about 4 hours, or until skins burst. After one hour, add salt, and fat (or salt pork). If necessary, add more hot water to keep the beans covered.

TO SERVE: Mash the beans to the consistency of mashed potatoes.

Frijoles Refritos

To Prepare Refried Beans:

Fry mashed cooked beans (see above) in 2 T. bacon fat or shortening until they are dry. Turn with spatula. Refried beans may be re-fried several times.

Canned Refried Beans:

Delicious refried beans may be bought in cans. Heat by frying as above. See Menu From Cans, page 56.

Serve with grated cheese and tostadas, or in

Bean Burros   below
Crisp and Flat Tacos   page 21
Enchiladas   page 28

Bean Burros

Use flour Tortillas de Harina (may be purchased ready-to-use at a Mexican store or supermarket). If necessary to freshen them, see page 15. Fill the tortilla with re-fried beans or chile con carne, or *guacamole* (page 37), or cheese, OR a combination of these. FOLD ends in and ROLL.

Soups (Sopas)

There are two kinds of soup in Mexico . . . *SOPA AGUADA, or liquid soup* as we know it, and *SOPA SECA, dry soup*. One of the dry soups, *SOPA DE PASTA,* served at *comida corrida,* their midday meal, is often made of vermicelli, noodles, or alphabet letters that have been slightly browned before being cooked in broth, not water. Garnish with cooked carrots and peas to add color.

Dry Rice Soup (6 servings)

(Sopa de Arroz) or Spanish Rice

We think of dry rice soup as a casserole, often called *SPANISH RICE*. The flavor is delightfully distinct, and offers a nice contrast to chile-seasoned foods.

3 T. fat
1 cup uncooked rice
1 medium onion, minced
1½ cups canned tomatoes

salt, to taste
2 T. carrot, minced
1 10½ oz. can beef or chicken broth
OR 2 cups meat stock

Brown the rice in hot fat. Add rest of ingredients, cover, and cook slowly until liquid is absorbed, about 25 minutes.

WHY DON'T YOU . . . FREEZE portions to serve as side dishes with your Mexican food (before serving, steam the rice, but do not add liquid) . . . DOUBLE THE RECIPE and save to stuff bell peppers. Add sausage, if desired.

Vegetable Soups

Vegetable soups are popular in Mexico . . . avocado, squash, or tomato. Cook the vegetable, mash, and add to hot meat broth, or milk. Season to taste.

For Chick Pea Soup, see recipe, page 36.

Sopa de Chile Verde (4 servings)

1 10½ oz. can beef broth
1 can water
1 medium onion, thinly sliced

1 green chile (canned)
grated cheese to garnish

Continued

Dilute beef broth with 1 can water. Simmer broth and onion about 10 minutes. Rinse the green chile, remove seeds and membrane. Chop the green chile and add to liquid. TO SERVE: add a little grated cheese to each portion.

Chick Pea Soup (12 servings)

1 lb. chick peas
2 qts. water
1 small onion, chopped
2 cups meat broth
(*Spanish variation*)

OR

2 cups milk
salt and pepper to taste

Soak chick peas in water overnight. Boil in same water until tender. Peel, grind, and pass through a colander. Brown the onion in butter. Add onion, meat broth or milk, and seasonings to chick pea broth, and simmer for 15 minutes.

Variation Using Meat Broth . . .

Cook as above but don't grind chick peas. Add 1 cup strained tomatoes and small pieces of ham to the meat broth. Simmer for 15 minutes.

Cheese (Queso)

The Mexicans use goat cheese in their recipes. Goats are plentiful there because they are well adapted to the country. MONTEREY or JACK CHEESE has a similar flavor to goat cheese. Use your *favorite* cheese in preparing Mexican food . . . CHEDDAR is very good. Some people substitute dry cottage cheese for crumbled goat cheese.

36

Avocados (Aguacates)

Avocados are plentiful and inexpensive in Mexico . . . nutritious, too, for they contain many vitamins and minerals. Avocados are used in salads often combined with other vegetables. Delicious with sections of grapefruit topped with French dressing . . . or stuffed with tuna salad, or sardines, or deviled eggs. For avocado soup, see page 35.

Guacamole

GUACAMOLE is a very popular spread made of mashed avocados. There are many recipes for *guacamole*. We prefer this simple one . . . the amount obtained will vary depending on the size of fruit and vegetables used.

1 large avocado	juice of lemon (lemon
1 small green chile	juice, or vinegar,
1 small tomato,	must always be
peeled	added to keep the
1 small onion	avocado from turn-
salt to taste	ing dark)

Mash all ingredients to consistency of butter. TO SERVE: spread GUACAMOLE on crisp tortillas or potato chips. Use also in soft and rolled tacos, page 21.

Vegetables (Legumbres)

Great quantities of corn, beans, peppers, rice, tomatoes, green tomatoes (small, but ripe), and onions are consumed in tortillas, tacos, soups, enchiladas.

The Mexicans also like peas, string beans, carrots, cauliflower, squash, and artichokes.

Squash With Cheese (4 servings)
(Calabacitas con Queso)

1 T. fat	4 squash, sliced
3 fresh green onions, chopped	(summer, zucchini, or scalloped)
2 fresh tomatoes, peeled, sliced	salt and pepper to taste
	⅓ cup cubed cheese

Brown onions in fat in heavy sauce pan. Add tomatoes, cover tightly, and cook over low heat for 3 minutes. Add squash and seasoning. Cover again and cook slowly for 20 minutes until squash is tender. Do not add water. Just before serving, add cubed cheese. Cover, turn off fire; cheese will melt.

String Beans with Red Chile Sauce
(Ejotes con Chile Colorado)

Use canned, frozen or freshly *cooked* green string beans. Add one can Red Chile Sauce and small pieces of crisp bacon. Cook 5 to 10 minutes. If desired, thicken the Red Chile Sauce slightly.

Savory Carrots (Zanahorias Sabrosas)

Marinate cooked, sliced carrots in 1 T. melted butter, seasoned with oregano and onion salt. Pan-fry with a little fat in skillet. Garnish with sifted toasted crumbs.

Nopal Cactus (Nopalitos)

A popular vegetable in Mexico is the very tender leaf of the NOPAL CACTUS. These are chopped, boiled, and served with sauces or eggs. This vegetable is also available in cans.

The fruit of the Nopal, called TUNAS (prickly pear) is red or green colored, full of seeds and juicy. These tunas are also used in making a beverage called COLONCHE.

The Nopal Cactus is on the flag of Mexico as part of the legend of the eagle and the locating of the Capitol.

Chick Peas (Garbanzos)

Good tasting chick peas can be bought in cans. Serve with butter as a vegetable.

Dried chick peas are starchy and should be soaked overnight. They must be boiled quite a while; if additonal water is needed, add hot water. You may want to peel off the little hulls.

Meats (Carnes)

There are several kinds of meat used by the Mexicans that are interesting for us to know about . . . *CARNE SECA* is dried beef, called *jerky* in the Southwest — drying preserves it . . . *CHICHARONES* are cracklings, the crisp rind of roasted pork . . . *CHORIZO*, sausage, highly spiced with garlic and chile sauce. The Mexicans use KIDNEYS, BRAINS, LIVER, or HEART boiled and usually served with tomato or chile sauce. There are interesting recipes, too, one you might *not* like, called *MENUDO*, boiled tripe . . . *ALBONDIGAS*, meatballs, but we think you have your favorite recipe . . . *MOLE*, a very dark sauce made of chile sauce, spices, and chocolate, is served over meat or fowl, especially turkey. See page 26.

40

Tamale Pie with Corn Meal

(serves 8-10)

Here is a casserole recipe you will like, even though it is not authentically Mexican. *It is quite mildly flavored, so if you want to pep it up, add a little hot chile sauce and oregano.*

1 T. fat
1 lb. lean ground beef
1 medium onion, chopped
1 clove of garlic, minced
1 large can tomatoes (No. 2½)

1 can whole kernel corn, (No. 303) drained
1½ T. chile powder
1½ t. salt
½ cup yellow corn meal
¾ cup milk
2 eggs
¾ cup ripe olives, drained, pitted

Brown ground beef, onion, and clove of garlic slowly in large skillet. Add tomatoes, corn, chile powder and salt. Simmer for 15 minutes, turn off heat. Add the corn meal, milk, eggs, and olives, *stirring thoroughly after each.* Pour into casserole and bake 45 minutes to 1 hour at 350°. WHY DON'T YOU . . . BAKE and SERVE it in a colorful MEXICAN POTTERY BOWL?

Variation, Using Tamale Dough:

Prepare ½ the recipe for Tamale dough, page 30. Use half the dough to line a pan or bowl. Make same filling as above, but omit the corn. Use remainder of dough as a top crust. Bake 45 minutes to 1 hour at 350°. Cut, and serve with Red Chile Sauce (Enchilada Sauce).

41

Poultry

chicken	(Pollo)
hen	(Gallina)
duck	(Pato)
turkey	(Guajolote)
pigeon	(Pichon)

Poultry is popular in Mexico and is served mostly in stews, with *mole* (page 26), or chile sauces (page 25). It is cut in large pieces and boiled. The broth is used for the sauces or saved for soups.

Eggs (Huevos)

Eggs are used everywhere in Mexico . . . fried, poached, hard-boiled, scrambled, omelets . . . in desserts (page 46) such as *Almendrado, Flan,* floating island, custards, and in baked or fried cookies. The yolk is compressed in chocolate tablets (beverages, page 43). Beaten eggs make a dip for vegetables. Even egg shells are used (page 60).

Rancher's Eggs (Huevos Rancheros) serves 4

This is a well-known breakfast recipe:

1 T. fat	salt and pepper
1 small onion chopped	4 eggs
2 canned green chiles, chopped	4 tortillas fried crisp (tostadas)
1 cup strained tomatoes and liquid	

Brown onion and chiles in fat. Add tomatoes and seasonings, and bring to a boil. Fry the eggs.

42

TO SERVE: Place an egg on each tortilla and cover with the sauce.

Variation:

Break the whole eggs into the sauce and poach. Serve on the tortillas and top with the sauce.

Fish (Pescado)

Fresh water and ocean sea foods are a favorite in Mexico. Every locality has its own recipes using local fish, although they are available throughout the country. Pan-fry or bake with tomato sauce (with or without chile). And make soup of the tail and head!

Beverages (Bebidas)

CHOCOLATE, the native drink, so impressed the Spanish Conquistadores that Cortés sent the cacao bean back to Spain as a curio.

The Mexican chocolate drink has egg yolk to thicken it, as well as vanilla, cinnamon, nutmeg, almonds, and is beaten to a froth . . . Compressed chocolate tablets can now be bought in Mexican stores . . . COFFEE is prepared very strong, and served with boiling milk (*leche*) . . . TEA is made from a variety of herbs or tree leaves boiled and sweetened with honey (*miel*) or brown sugar (*piloncillo* or *panocha*). FRUIT ADES such as limeade, orangeade, lemonade are popular . . . *ATOLE* is corn gruel made with variations of milk and fruit juices . . . *CHAMPURRADO* is made of masa, chocolate, spices . . . *AGUAMIEL* is the fresh juice of the maguey cactus and is often fed to babies.

Coffee (Café)

To Prepare Coffee Extract:
Make very strong drip (preferably) or boiled coffee.

To Serve:
Add 2 T. coffee extract or more to suit taste to 1 cup very hot milk. Sweeten with sugar. It will be a rich tan color . . . in fact, the Spanish word for tan is CAFE CON LECHE!

Tea (Té)

Spiced Tea Extract
Simmer in 1 quart water . . .

9 whole cloves
6 berries of allspice
1 1" stick cinnamon

1 lemon, slices and juice

Strain

To Serve:
Add as much of the spiced tea extract as you like to hot or cold tea. Sugar to taste.

Chocolate

On Mexican Menus, Spanish Chocolate will have egg in it; French Chocolate will be very thick with corn starch.

To Prepare Chocolate:
Using Cocoa: (2 servings)

1 t. cocoa or more to suit taste
1 t. sugar
salt
½ cup water

1 ½ cups milk
1 egg, well-beaten
pinch of cinnamon
pinch of nutmeg if desired

Continued

Mix cocoa, sugar, salt, water and bring to a boil. Slowly add milk, well-beaten egg, and spices, and beat again. Use beater or *molinillo* until it is foaming. Serve hot.

Using Mexican Chocolate or Tablets:

Add 1 square Mexican chocolate or tablet to 1 cup scalded milk. Use beater or *molinillo* until it is frothy.

molinillo

Pinole

PINOLE, used in making *ATOLE,* is ground toasted corn with brown sugar (*piloncillo* or *panocha*). It looks like cocoa and may be bought in dry form in Mexican stores.

Atole

To Prepare An Individual Serving:
Mix to smooth paste:

> 1 T. pinole
> ¼ cup water

Add:

> ½ cup milk
> ¼ t. salt
> 1 t. sugar

Simmer for 8 minutes, stirring occasionally.

Desserts (Postres)

Since many Mexican foods are hot and heavy, the best complement for them is a light, cooling dessert such as *NIEVE* (snow), ice cream, or *HELADO,* sherbet. GELATIN DESSERTS are very popular and were introduced into Mexico by the Spaniards. The most unusual use of gelatin by the Mexicans is in *ALMEN-DRADO,* see page 48.

The Mexicans also like assorted fruits for dessert served on a tray with everyone choosing his favorite ... PAPAYA, oval like a melon, pumpkin color, peach flavor ... MANGOES, yellow-red color, thick skin, juicy, pulp, strong apricot flavor ... *ZAPOTES,* very dark color, sweet as honey ... *POMEGRANATES,*

WATERMELON (*sandía*), *CANTALOUPE* (*melón*), BANANAS (*plátanos*) — there are many varieties . . . and COCOANUT (*coco*), PINEAPPLE (*piña*), ORANGES (*naranjas*), CHERRIES (*cerezas*), FIGS (*higos*), PEARS (*peras*), *GUAYAVA*. PRESERVED FRUIT (*pastas de frutas*) is served sliced as we serve fruit cake.

Caramel Custard (Flan)   (4-6 servings)

(Prepared powdered *FLAN* can be bought in stores in Mexico. Just add milk and bring to a boil.)

Burnt Sugar Topping

4 T. sugar

Heat the sugar in a small skillet until light brown syrup forms. Spread evenly on sides and bottom of custard cups while still hot.

Custard

2 cups milk	pinch of salt
4 eggs, beaten	½ t. vanilla
2 level T. sugar	

Scald the milk, then slowly add the eggs, sugar, salt, and vanilla. Pour into the sugared custard cups and set them in a pan of hot water. Bake at 350° for 30 minutes, or until a knife inserted into custard comes out clean. TO SERVE FLAN: loosen custards and turn out so that the burnt sugar tops the custard. Serve cold.

Almendrado

The most delightful
of Mexican desserts
is *ALMENDRADO*.
In the Mexican na-
tional colors of red,
white, and green, it
gives a perfect finish
to any meal. We

also like to serve it as a party dessert. This recipe serves
8-10 and may be prepared a day ahead.

1½ envelopes gelatin   ½ t. vanilla
½ cup cold water   ½ t. almond extract
¼ cup boiling water   pinch of salt
6 egg whites   red and green food
½ cup sugar   coloring

Soak the gelatin in cold water. Add boiling water and
stir to dissolve. Cool. Beat egg whites stiff and add the
sugar, *alternating* with the gelatin liquid, using electric mixer at high speed. Add vanilla, almond, and
salt. *Be sure* to whip *thoroughly* so the gelatin *blends
completely* with the egg whites (if you don't, it will
separate when chilled). It should look fluffy, and will
make about 2 quarts of "foam." Divide mixture into
3 parts, leaving 1 part white, tinting the others red and
green to resemble the Mexican flag. Pour the 3 layers
(red, white, green) into oblong loaf pan. Chill.

Almendrado Sauce (a thin custard)

2 T. cornstarch   6 egg yolks
1 T. cold milk   ½ t. vanilla
2 cups scalded milk   ½ t. almond extract
½ cup sugar   sliced toasted almonds
pinch of salt   to garnish

Dissolve cornstarch in cold milk. Add to scalded milk, sugar, and salt. Boil until slightly thickened, stirring constantly. Beat egg yolks, vanilla and almond extracts. Slowly add to hot mixture and let it simmer until slightly thickened, stirring constantly (takes just a minute). Chill.
SERVE COLORFUL ALMENDRADO in squares, and top with the SAUCE and sliced toasted almonds.

Bread Pudding (Capirotada) serves 6

2 cups milk	1/3 cup raisins
4 cups bread, toasted, diced	1/3 cup peanuts
	1/3 cup cheese, diced
3/4 cup brown sugar	1/4 t. salt
1/3 cup melted butter	1 t. cinnamon

Combine all ingredients. Pour into greased 1 1/2 quart casserole. Bake at 350° for 45 minutes. Serve hot or cold.

Floating Island (Isla Flotante) serves 6

2 egg yolks	1/4 t. salt
1 whole egg	1 1/3 cups scalded milk
1/3 cup sugar	1 t. vanilla

In top of double boiler, beat egg yolks and 1 whole egg. Add sugar, salt, and scalded milk. Stir constantly until custard coats spoon. Add vanilla and pour into bowl or individual dishes.

Topping

2 egg whites   1/4 cup sugar

Beat egg whites and fold in sugar. This topping goes

on in peaks or "islands" while custard is hot. Cool before serving.

A Tart Dessert (Postre Delicia) serves 8

1 envelope gelatin
½ cup cold orange juice
½ cup boiling orange juice
1 cup canned crushed

pineapple, drained
1 cup apple sauce
1 cup shredded cocoanut, lightly packed

Dissolve gelatin in cold orange juice, then add boiling orange juice. Add pineapple, apple sauce, and shredded cocoanut. Mix well, and pour into custard cups.

Meringue

2 egg whites   2 T. sugar
¼ t. cream of tartar

Beat egg whites with cream of tartar until foamy. Gradually add sugar, beating until peaks are formed. Pour meringue over top of fruit, and brown in broiler or oven. Serve cold.

Buñuelos (Very thin fried cookies)

At Christmastime, it is traditional to serve BUÑUE-LOS! Break them into a bowl and add a thin syrup made of brown sugar (*piloncillo* or *panocha*) flavored with a stick of cinnamon.

2 eggs
¼ cup milk
2 T. melted butter
2 cups flour

½ T. sugar
½ t. salt
Sugar mixed with cinnamon to sprinkle on top.

Beat eggs, add milk and melted butter. Sift flour, sugar, and salt, and add to first ingredients. Make into 1" balls. Press them into very thin circles on a floured board. Deep fry until golden brown. Sprinkle with sugar mixed with cinnamon.

Turnovers (Empanadas)

SWEET *EMPANADAS* are turnovers made of pastry filled with your favorite jam, thick apple sauce, or pumpkin. Bake in hot oven for 25 minutes.

For MEAT *EMPANADAS*, fill turnovers with meat or chicken, Bake as Above.

Mexican Wedding Cookies (Polvorones)

These are "little dusted ones," from the Spanish, *polvo,* dust.

½ cup butter
½ cup shortening
1 t. vanilla
2 cups flour, sifted
¾ cup finely chopped
   nuts

½ cup powdered
  sugar to dust
  cookies

Cream butter, shortening, and vanilla. Add flour and nuts. Shape into small balls, and place on ungreased cooky sheet. Bake in hot oven, 425°, about 10 minutes. Dust in powdered sugar while still warm.

Mexican Candy

Mexican children satisfy their "sweet tooth" by chewing on sugar canes. Visitors to Mexico remember the picturesque street vendor with his pushcart on which he displays his wares — appetizing and colorful candies.

Cactus Candy

Cubes of Barrel Cactus	1 T. slaked lime to
Water to cover cubes	each quart of water
Sugar (equal to amount	used (buy lime at
of cactus cubes)	drugstore)

First, find a friend who owns a barrel cactus and who wouldn't mind your using it! Use a hatchet to chop off all the ribs and to remove green coating from the pulp. Cut the pulp into cubes. Let cubes stand overnight in water to which lime has been added.

The next morning wash cubes thoroughly in several clear waters. Boil cubes in water until clear and transparent. Drain thoroughly. Measure equal amounts of sugar and cubes and boil gently until sugar is absorbed. Roll in granulated sugar.

Mexican Pralines

2 cups brown sugar　　1 T. butter
¼ cup light cream　　1 cup pecans

Stir sugar, cream, and butter over heat until sugar is dissolved. Add pecans. Boil without stirring to soft ball stage (235°). Remove from heat. Stir until mixture starts to thicken. Drop from teaspoon on waxed paper.

Cocada (Cocoanut Candy)

2 cups sugar　　　½ cup cocoanut
½ cup milk　　　½ cup nutmeats
1 T. butter　　　1 t. vanilla

Combine sugar, milk, and butter. Stir constantly over heat until soft ball stage (235°) is reached. Remove from fire, add vanilla, cocoanut, and nutmeats. Drop from teaspoon on waxed paper.

Fruit Peel

Peel of 4 large oranges,　Water to cover peel
　cut in strips (may　1 T. salt
　also use grapefruit　2 cups sugar
　or lemon or lime peel)

Soak peel overnight in salted water. The next day drain thoroughly and wash peel. Cover peel with cold water and bring slowly to boiling. Drain. Repeat boiling three times using fresh cold water each time. Drain thoroughly.

Add sugar to peel. Add a little water, if necessary, and stir to dissolve sugar. Cook slowly until peel is translucent. Drain. Roll in granulated sugar. Spread to dry on wire rack.

Have your guests fill and stack their own like flap-jacks! There's your whole meal! See page 28.

Little Masa Cakes (6 cakes)

1 cup Masa (or Masa Harina)	1 can Red Chile Sauce chopped onion, grated
1/4 t. salt	cheese to garnish
1 t. baking powder	

Mix Masa, salt, and baking powder. Shape into balls, then flatten into 3″ cakes. Deep fry (can be done in as little as 1/2″ fat). Serve covered with heated Red Chile Sauce (Enchilada Sauce), grated cheese and chopped onion.

FOR VARIETY, try these LITTLE QUICKIES ... filling and tasty with a parched corn flavor. Makes 6.

1 cup corn meal	1/4 t. salt
1 T. enriched flour	1 can Red Chile
1/2 cup water	Sauce

Mix corn meal, flour, and water. Shape into cakes (may be crumbly to handle). Fry on well-seasoned griddle in small amount of fat. Serve covered with heated Red Chile Sauce (Enchilada Sauce).

54

Menu
from cans

Enchiladas
Tacos
Frijoles Refritos
Helado
(Sherbet)

TORTILLAS — fry

RED CHILI SAUCE — heat

fry

grate

chop

REFRIED BEANS — heat in fat

Enchiladas (page 27)

Fry tortilla

Dip in sauce

Sprinkle with cheese

Top with sauce, cheese, chopped onion

Heat in pan in oven

Tacos (page 20)

Fold
Fry until crisp
Fill with meat, cheese,

Refried Beans (page 33)

Top with cheese
onion, lettuce, Red
Chile Sauce.

Are you using your...

Mexican pottery bowls? Wonderful for casseroles! After all, these are Mexican utensils. Some people season them with hot fat the first time they use them ...

Continued

Set your table with d e c o r a t i v e Mexican handmade articles. It's the ir-regularities t h a t m a k e t h e m so charming.

Mexican Fun
Breaking the Piñata

Breaking the Piñata is a game for birthday parties in Mexico . . . and always at Christmas.

A *piñata* is made from an *olla* or clay jar filled with candy or small gifts, decorated gaily with ruffled crepe paper to resemble a flower, a bird, a lamb, a frog, or even *El Toro,* the bull.

At the party, hang the *piñata* from the ceiling. Your guests will take turns trying to break it . . .

But first, they will be blindfolded and twirled around 3 times, then allowed 3 strikes with a stick.

What fun . . . as the rest of the guests swing the *p i ñ a t a* out of reach! When the *piñata* breaks . . . what a scramble!

Beautiful *piñatas* can be bought in Mexico a n d the United States OR you can make your own . . . even a paper bag filled with wrapped candy or nuts can be a *piñata*.

Cascarones

Cascarones, elaborately decorated eggshells filled with confetti, are fun at Easter in Mexico. The game is to crush the *cascarón* on someone's head before he can do it to you!

Luminarios

Light at a Mexican Fiesta may be candles in paper lanterns, or even a big bonfire or *luminario*.

For decorations at Christmas, make your own *luminarios* by putting a candle in sand in a paper sack! Outline your home, your walks, your roof with them . . . they shed a beautifully soft, warm glow!

Spanish Pronunciation

The Spanish alphabet is like the English alphabet with these four letters added:

ch as in church
ñ as in canyon

rr as a trilled r
ll as in William

Vowels are pronounced clearly and distinctly.

a as in ah!
e as in let
i as in see

o as in or
u as in rule
y as in boy

Consonants W and K are omitted
           H is always silent
           B and V are pronounced alike
           J is like H in English

Accent: Words ending in vowels or N or S, have their accent on the next to last syllable.

Words ending in a consonant other than N or S, have their accent on the last syllable.

Exceptions to above will have a written accent.

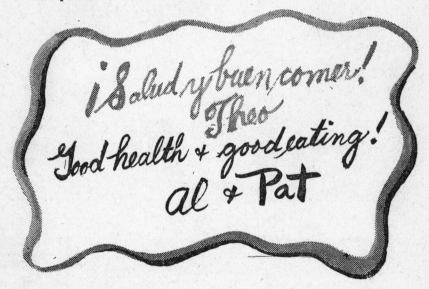

¡Salud y buen comer!
Theo

Good health + good eating!
al + Pat

NOTES